Spitfire, Merlin Variant

Written by Ron Mackay

Walk Around®

Squadron Signal Publications

Cover Art by Don Greer

Line Illustrations by Todd Sturgell

(Front Cover) The National markings on these two Mk. I Spitfires of No. 609 Squadron are restricted to Type B wing and fuselage roundels. The serial number is applied to the upper fin. Black/white undersides were a feature between 1938 and 1940.

(Back Cover) USAAF Maj. Garth Jared was 309FS CO between 9 November 1943 and 18 April 1944 when he was killed in combat. His personal Mk IX bears his initials (GJ) as codes in white. Camouflage is Dark earth and Middle stone above with Azure blue undersides.

About the Walk Around® Series

The Walk Around® series is about the details of specific military equipment using color and black-and-white archival and photographs of in-service, preserved, and restored equipment. *Walk Around*® titles are devoted to aircraft and military vehicles. These are picture books focus on operational equipment, not one-off or experimental subjects.

Squadron/Signal Walk Around® books feature the best surviving and restored historic aircraft and vehicles. Inevitably, the requirements of preservation, restoration, exhibit, and continued use may affect these examples in some details of paint and equipment. Authors strive to highlight any feature that departs from original specifications.

Proudly printed in the U.S.A.
Copyright 2013 Squadron/Signal Publications
1115 Crowley Drive, Carrollton, TX 75006-1312 U.S.A.
www.SquadronSignalPublications.com

Hardcover ISBN 978-0-89747-731-4
Softcover ISBN 978-0-89747-732-1

Military/Combat Photographs and Snapshots

If you have any photos of aircraft, armor, soldiers, or ships of any nation, particularly wartime snapshots, please share them with us and help make Squadron/Signal's books all the more interesting and complete in the future. Any photograph sent to us will be copied and returned. Electronic images are preferred. The donor will be fully credited for any photos used. Please send them to the address above.

(Title Page) Mk. Vb ER622/WR: B (with clipped wings) from No. 40 (SAAF) Squadron is seen at Qâbis (Gabes), Tunisia, during April 1943. Camouflage of Dark earth, Middle stone and Azure blue underneath was standard for the Mediterranean Theater of Operations.

Acknowledgments

The prime credit for this book has to go to Jerry Scutts. He first introduced me to Squadron/Signal back in 1980 whose owner he persuaded to grant me my first of numerous subsequent commissions, namely *Lancaster in Action.* Jerry's superb rendition of the *'In Action'* book on the Spitfire and his sadly-premature death several years back are the twin catalysts in my embarking on the project. The photographic material is drawn from several private sources that maintain Spitfires in airworthy condition in the United Kingdom. I thank the staff concerned for access to these aircraft.

Introduction

The Supermarine Spitfire rightly occupies a pre-eminent place in the 20th Century history of Great Britain. The entry of the Spitfire, along with its Hurricane stable-mate, into combat in the early stages of World War II ensured that democracy's "ever-fragile flower" would be able to sustain itself in the face of the Nazi steam-roller that had hitherto crushed that spirit within Western Europe. The 1940 Battle of Britain could not have been sustained without the Hurricane but victory over the Luftwaffe would have been problematical without the Spitfire's equal presence.

The lithe, Spitfire fighter design progressed in terms of engine and striking power over the ensuing five years of tragedy and triumph to spread its influence around the globe, even over the ocean in the form of the Seafire variant. The posthumous legacy that Reginald Mitchell bequeathed to the Nation with his superlative design still evokes an instant sense of individual and corporate pride when the word "Spitfire" is mentioned. It is simply an icon of Britain's military tradition.

The deceptively frail airframe accommodated a number of structural and power advances that at first sight should have overwhelmed its progress in its primary role as a superiority fighter. Not only was the airframe fitted with ever more up-rated engine power-plants that more than doubled in output during WWII; but it was slung with a multitude of armament variations, extending from bombs to rockets. The single and regrettable limitation on overall performance was the paucity of internal fuel capacity. But for this shortcoming, the Spitfire could have joined its USAAF contemporaries in besting the Luftwaffe over the Reich. As it was, however, the Spitfire was forced to operate on the geographic fringes of Europe.

The advent of the jet-age towards the end of WWII ensured that the Spitfire and its propeller-driven contemporaries would soon be relegated to the annals of aviation history. Nevertheless, service with RAF Auxiliary Squadrons ensured that the Spitfire's presence would still be felt for several years after its finest hours in WWII. The Arab-Israeli battles of 1948 and the Malayan Crisis witnessed its use in an offensive role, although these were relatively exceptional post-War cases.

Today the Spitfire still graces the modern-day skies at air displays around the globe. The Battle of Britain Memorial Flight regularly dispatches one of its several examples of the Supermarine design, along with a Lancaster and Hurricane. All three aircraft thereby serve to symbolize the spirit of the Nation in former adversity – the Spitfire and Hurricane representing National defiance in its darkest hour and the Lancaster the kernel of effective striking power against one of the most pernicious and autocratic of philosophies attempting to bar the progress of modern humanity.

The Supermarine design enjoyed such a long career and went through so many Marks during its lifetime that comprehensive coverage of the topic would more than fill out a bulky, voluminous tome. The present compact volume is therefore limited exclusively to coverage of those airframes that accommodated the Rolls/Royce Merlin engine as their power-source. Also excluded from this book due to considerations of space are the Fleet Air Arm's Seafire variations.

The technically pure outline of the Spitfire is seen in this side-view of a Mk. 1. This aircraft, P 9450, was one of 181 airframes delivered between January and August 1940 and assigned to No. 64 Squadron from which it went missing in action (MIA) on 5 December. Fuselage markings are limited to the Type A roundel.

This Spitfire re-build bears a mix of markings officially issued around May 1940. Type A1 fin flash and Type A1 fuselage roundel with thin yellow surround are evident but there are no squadron letters. There is a red-edged yellow gas-detection diamond on the port wing surface. Serial P9374 refers to a 92 Squadron fighter listed MIA on 25 May 1940.

AR213 is a late-production MK. I turned out by the Yeovil-based Westland Co. in mid-1941. Its use was limited to training, since the Mk. V was in full operational service by this stage of WWII. It bears Dark green and Dark earth top and "Sky S" lower camouflage, with Type A1 fin flashes and fuselage roundels.

AR213's aerial wire extends back from the mast to an "inverted-L" metal frame that is riveted to the top of the rudder structure. The wire traces into the center of the horizontal section.

The separation-line between the main fuselage and the tail section can be seen running in a forward-angled manner. The inspection panel at the fuselage base is the port-side fitting that provides access to the rudder control-cable lever structure.

AR213's starboard wing leading edge indicates the wide spacing of the inner and outer machine guns with red-doped aperture patches. The wider weapon-spread and more flexible wing structure compared to the Hurricane presented the pilot with a greater degree of difficulty in accurately landing his gunfire upon another aircraft.

An underside view of the starboard wingtip on AR213 picks out the trestle stencil. Also seen are two of a number of W/T stencils on the airframe. These refer to the need to bond the flight control surfaces to prevent static electricity build-up; the action also enhances radio transmission and reception. All wording is applied in black.

AR213's propeller blade shape is different from the other examples in this book and is probably a Jablo-produced DeHaviland designed unit. The spinner cover is shorter and more bulbous, reflecting the pattern in use during the first part of WWII. It is retained in place by nine screws, three in each of the spaces between the propeller blades.

The Mk. Vb's spinner cover is similar in pattern to the Mk. IX with a small blunt tip. However, the cover has small raised fairings on the front edge of the propeller apertures that are absent on the Mk. IX's cover.

A close-up of the spinner cover reveals the slot-connector for retaining or detaching the fitting. This system is simpler than the multi-screw layout exhibited by other spinner covers seen in the book. Stencilled instructions are applied in black.

Mk. Vb EP120 has the three-bladed constant-speed propeller variant introduced on the Mk. 1 in early 1940. The Mk. V used either the de Havilland 5/39 or Rotol RX 5/10 units. Both had constant-speed controls with different fine- and course-pitch settings for the blades, with 20 and 35 degrees variation respectively.

The Mk. Vb's engine compartment has a metal former centrally located at the top; this extends from the vertical frame behind the glycol tank back to the firewall. It acts as a stiffener for the top cowling panel.

The Mk. Vb's Merlin 45/55 Series engine block was shorter in length than that on the Merlin 60 Series. The bearer frame has an extra diagonal support extending down from the engine support member, to which the radio suppressor box is attached.

By contrast Mk.Vb Spitfire BM597 features the revised pattern for the engine exhaust shrouds. All three orifices are crimped in a narrower 'fish-tail' shape. The "boost" effect of the exhaust outflow marginally increased aircraft speed.

EP120 has the distinctive three-part engine exhaust shroud that was a feature on Spitfires up to the Mk. VI variant. The surface is burnished metal in texture. The front and central orifices are "orange-slice" in shape and the rear one is round.

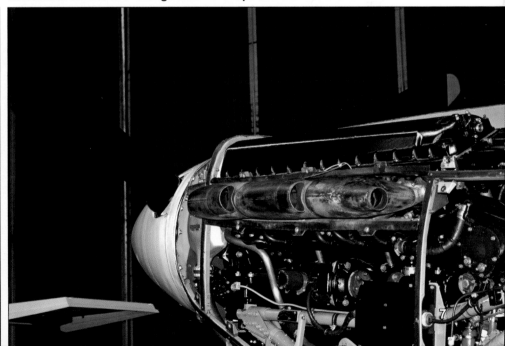

The carburetor air intake on BM597 lacks the fine-mesh screen with which to keep out foreign objects that would otherwise damage the unit. Engine starting plug cover is above with wording in black. Gun camera aperture is on port wing leading edge.

EP120's fuel compartment panel is detached, exposing the upper tank with a capacity of 48 Gallons. The tank is retained in place by pairs of quick-release pins, two of which are positioned in line with the dark panels at the base.

The hydraulic system's reservoir tank is mounted on the starboard face of the fire-proof bulkhead. A dipstick is incorporated into the filler-neck and is marked to indicate the maximum content-level.

The fuel compartment cover is also detached. The fuel-pipe is located under the forward end and the black stencil confirms the maximum fuel capacity (85 Gallons) and 100 Octane quality. The curved line on the rear edge fits in with the windshield base.

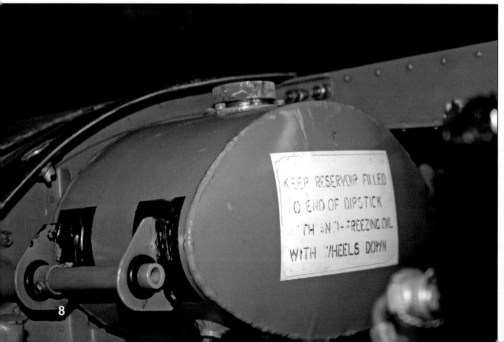

The rear section of the top cowling panel features the "D-pattern" access flap to the hydraulic oil reservoir. The three blister shapes accommodate engine fittings that extend above the panel surface. The small scoop is the air intake for the compressor.

The top engine cowling for the Mk. Vb is detached. It is normally retained in place by seven screws spaced out along the lower rim along with two at either end. The panel is tapered slightly down at its forward rim to line up with the spinner cover.

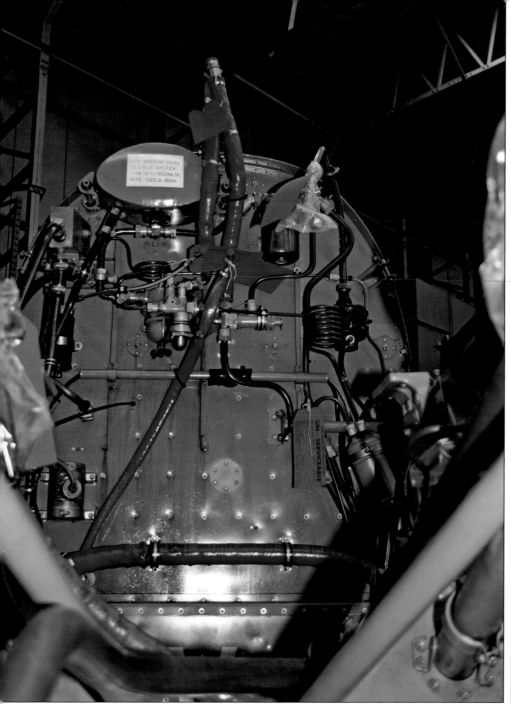

This head-on view of the fire-proofed bulkhead between the engine and the cockpit shows only the oil reservoir tank remaining in position. Most of the pipe-lengths are bronze with a silver finish applied to the fixed connector unit in the upper-center.

EP120's engine is detached to reveal the bearer frame's outline. The starboard section contains one of the glycol tank pipes that is bronze in color. The "inverted-U" main weight-bearing frame is clearly depicted. The frame is sprayed Interior grey-green.

Seen from the side, the EP120's engine bearer frame reveals the standard structure fitted to the Supermarine design. Overall frame-expansion proved subsequently necessary to fit the greater length of Series 60 engines first introduced on the Mk. VII.

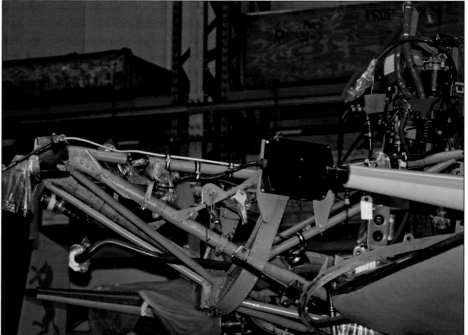

A general view of the Mk. Vb's inner wing area picks out the large fairing for the cannon's ammunition drum, the parallel raised runners to the inside and the flap indicator panel in the center foreground.

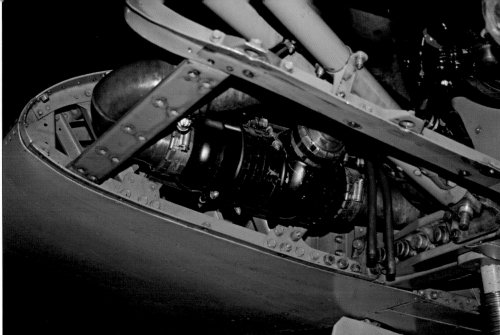

The Mk. Vb's cooling-system thermostat is in the leading edge of the starboard wing/fuselage junction. The unit is black with silver pipe-connectors. The pipe exiting at the back traces through the wing main-spar and into the top of the radiator.

The Spitfire's wing walk-way is a standard pattern with an anti-slip surface. The outer edge follows a straight fore-and-aft line; the inner edge is angled inwards from rear to front and matches the base-line of the wing fairing panel.

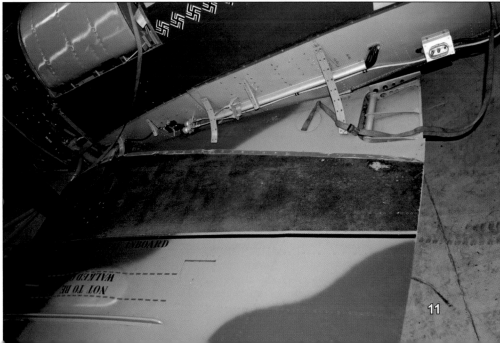

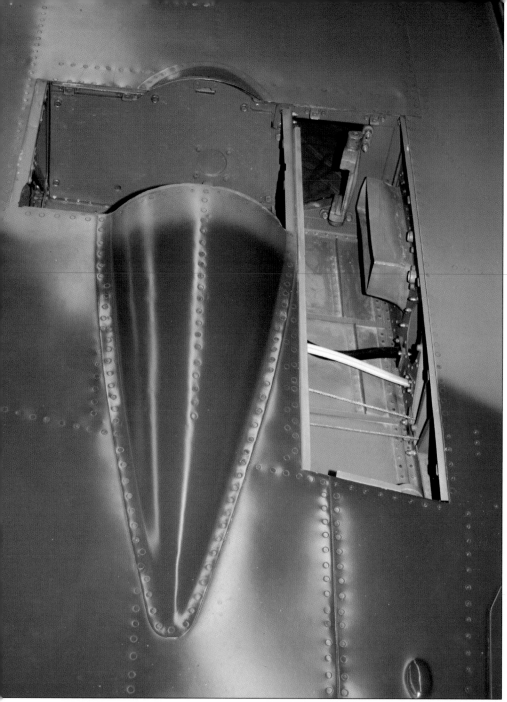

The black lines are indicators for personnel to refrain from walking on the more fragile main wing area. The lettering is in black, but the dotted lines on the bulged panel are red. The parallel raised strips are strengthening strakes for the wheel well that appear to be a specific feature on some standard and "clipped"-wing Mk. Vs.

The red-painted mast in line with the lateral walk-way stencil provides a visual indicator to the pilot when the landing gear is in the lowered position; it retracts when the gear is raised. A second visual indicator is set on the instrument panel's port side.

The Hispano cannon compartment panels ahead of and parallel to the ammunition drum fairing have here been detached. The chute positioned on the side of the right-hand compartment is the ejection feed for the cannon shell-cases.

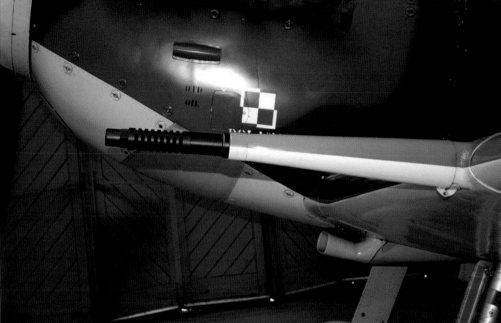

The EP120's cannon barrel sheaths comprise single units. These are attached via the top-mounted lug to the rectangular panel that is, in turn, slotted into the wing. The ammunition drums hold 60 rounds, but the belt-fed cannon on the Mk. Vc doubles this capacity.

The cannon barrel on Mk. V BM597 displays its exposed forward section as well as its overall extended length. The greater striking power of the 20mm shells was partially balanced-out by the reduced ammunition capacity compared to bullet-caliber weaponry.

The muzzle of the cannon barrel is clamped firmly within the sheath-cover by a large hexagonal-pattern nut. This reportedly prevents damage to the sheath that could occur from uncontrolled barrel vibration when firing the weapon.

The impression of relative fragility posed by the Spitfire's airframe is deceptive. Bomb-loads of up to 1,000 pounds featured on those aircraft assigned to fighter-bomber operations and often included USAAF 500-lb weapons as seen in this picture.

Spitfire Mk I Specifications

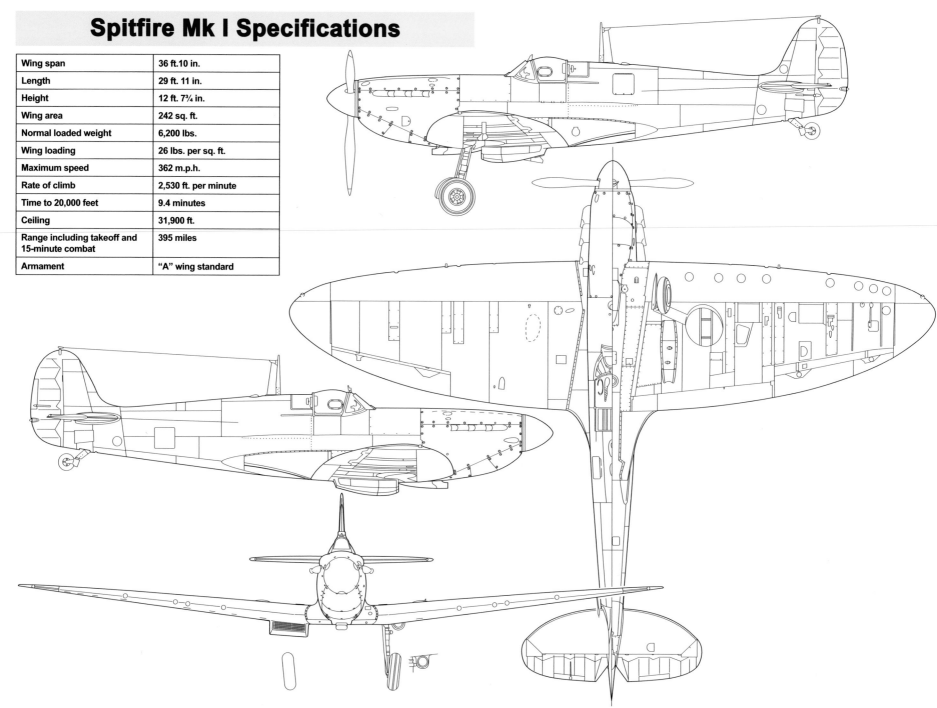

Wing span	36 ft.10 in.
Length	29 ft. 11 in.
Height	12 ft. 7¾ in.
Wing area	242 sq. ft.
Normal loaded weight	6,200 lbs.
Wing loading	26 lbs. per sq. ft.
Maximum speed	362 m.p.h.
Rate of climb	2,530 ft. per minute
Time to 20,000 feet	9.4 minutes
Ceiling	31,900 ft.
Range including takeoff and 15-minute combat	395 miles
Armament	"A" wing standard

Spitfire Mk Vb Specifications

Wing span	"B" wing 36 ft. 10 in.
Length	29 ft. 11 in.
Height	9 ft. 11 in.
Wing area	242 sq. ft.
Empty weight	5,065 lbs.
Normal loaded weight*	6,750 lbs.
Wing loading	26 lbs. per sq. ft.
Maximum speed	369 m.p.h. at 19,500 ft.
Normal cruising speed	272 m.p.h. at 5,000 ft.
Rate of climb	4,750 ft. per minute
Service ceiling	38,200 ft.
Absolute ceiling	36,700 ft.
Stalling speed at 6,400 lb weight	78 m.p.h. (flaps up) 70 m.p.h. (flaps down)
Armament	"B" wing standard, some "A" or "C"

*Maximum 6,710 lb bomb load limited to 500 lbs. for operations.

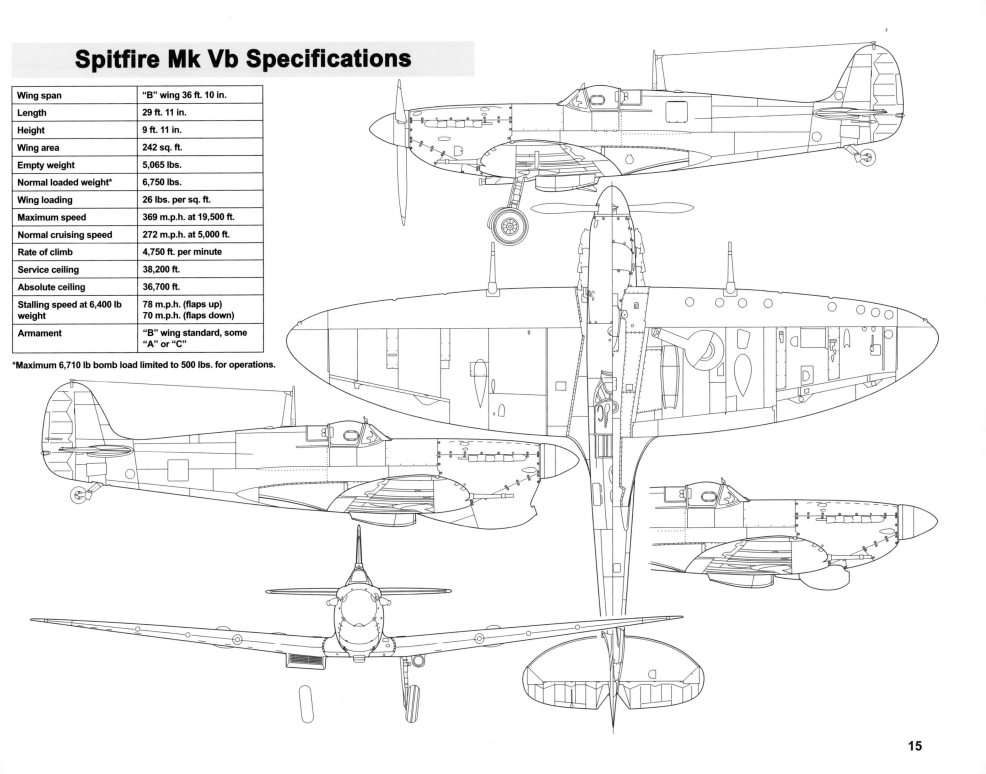

The outer machine gun mounting is located over the Type B roundel. The access panel has a ridge that covers the securing pin for the rear stirrup retaining the machine gun in place that would otherwise not fit in due to the wing's shallow depth at this point.

The inner machine gun's cover on the upper wing is shorter in length compared to the outer cover. The forward edge butts on to the joint line between the main and leading edge wing sections, which are separately manufactured and then linked up.

16

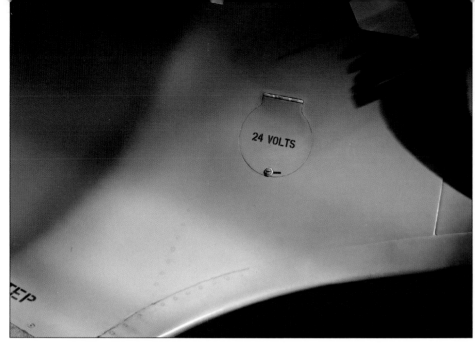

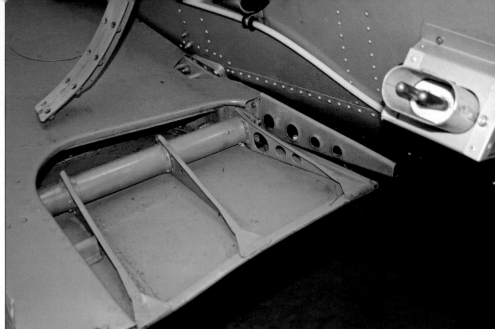

The access panel to the electrical and radio system ground socket on MH434 is hinged to open upwards and is secured by a single screw. The 24-Volt power reference on the panel is stencilled in black.

EP120's electrical and radio systems' ground socket unit's socket-pins protrude from an angled-out box structure, whose shape contrasts with the rounded mounting that is seen on MH434.

The port inner-wing on BM597 features a gun-camera whose aperture can be seen adjacent to the engine cowling. The camera's operation was synchronised with the gun's firing sequences but engine-vibration could affect the clarity of the developed film.

The rear pair of wing fairing panels on the Mk. Vb is seen here. The curved outer section that extends back from the wing trailing edge when the fairing is in place features a reinforcing strip.

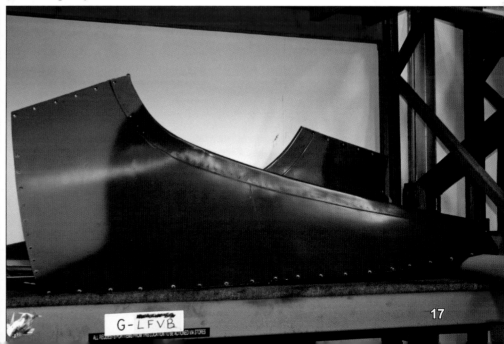

An angular view of the oil cooler fairing picks out the separation lines of the three-section frame. The rear section is raised upwards in a "scoop" shape.

This square detachable panel directly behind the outer rim of the landing-gear bay gives the ground crew access to the port-side flap's hydraulic jack. Three lever-ended screws retain the panel in place when it is closed.

The oil-cooler equipment on Spitfires up to the Mk.VI was mounted under the port wing, outboard of the landing gear strut. The tandem-linked units are housed in a slim fairing whose front end is circular. A wire-mesh screen is fitted over the cooler front.

The detaching of the oil cooler cover reveals the unit itself. The exterior has a burnt metal finish. The wire mesh front cover is repeated on the rear facing.

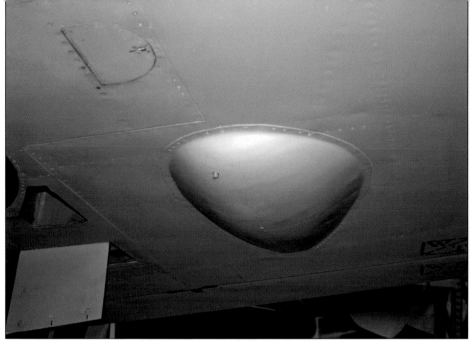

The expanded shape of the cannon ammunition drum is the reason for the 'teardrop' bulge fitted to the lower wing surfaces. The D-shaped panel at the top-left accesses the port landing lamp connections; the lamp is normally located in front of the 'teardrop' bulge but these were deleted on later-production batches.

The 'inverted L' slot for the outer machine gun's discharged bullet cases on the Mk. Vb is seen here. A similar slot applies to the inner weapon's discharged bullet cases but it is angled in the opposite direction.

The original radio mast, featured on initial production Spitfire airframes, was un-tapered in shape. It was displaced by an aerodynamically tapered-pattern mast during 1939.

This is a close-up of the aileron inner hinge on the port wing. The hinge pin's securing hexagonal nut is seen against the wing trailing-edge. Part of the aileron control lever, sprayed in Interior grey-green, appears out of the D-shaped access hole.

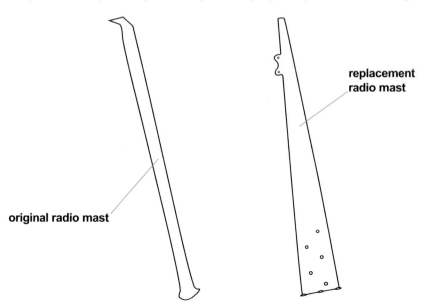

replacement radio mast

original radio mast

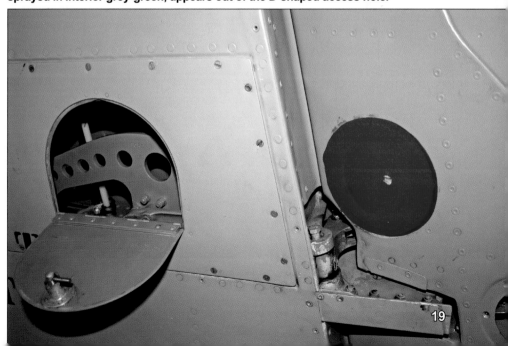

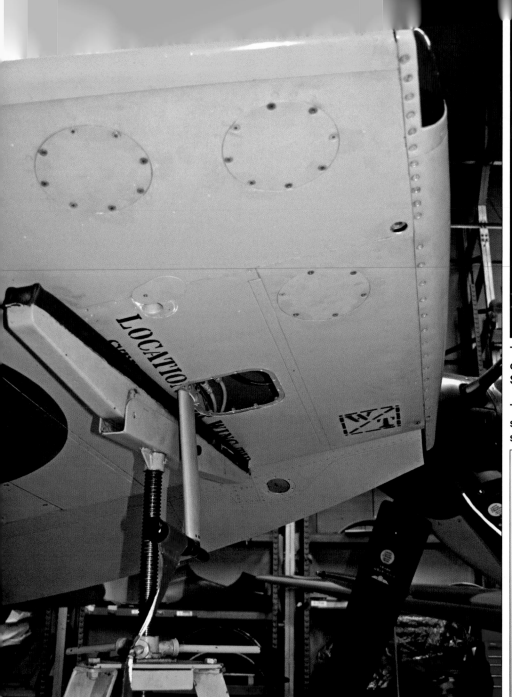

The wingtips of a number of Mk. V airframes were shortened in this manner. The result of the alteration was to increase the rate of roll, although the overall performance of this Spitfire variant was still dangerously inferior to that of the Fw 190.

This wheel bay on a Mk. V displays a silver finish but normal practice was for it to be sprayed in Interior grey-green. The plain overall surfaces are only broken by thin metal strips criss-crossing the roof.

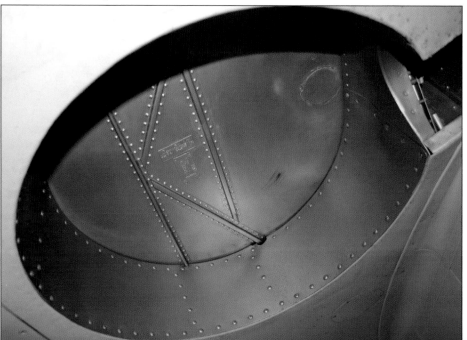

The end-on view of the "clipped" wing surface demonstrates how the navigation light mountings are altered from the original circular unit that extended beyond the leading edge to one whose Plexiglas outer edge is flush with the wing-tip surface.

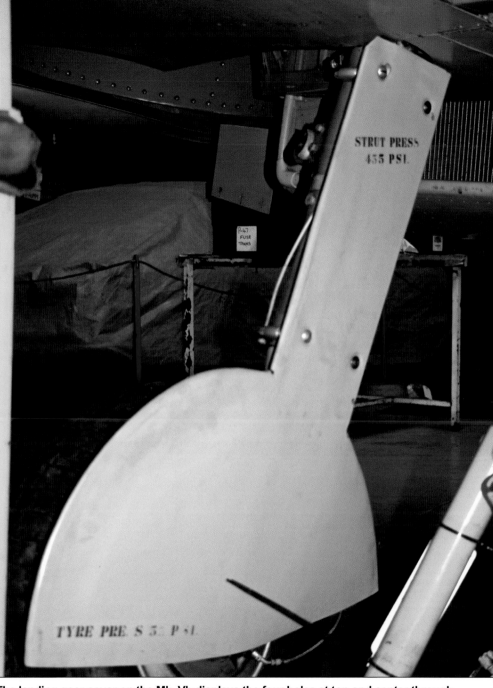

The Mk. V landing gear struts lack the triangular anti-torque frame located at the lower-front of the struts; these first appeared on later batches of the Mk. IX, as seen on MH434. The thin locking rod angles across the lower-front surface of the strut. Note the square-treaded wheel surface.

The landing gear cover on the Mk. Vb displays the four holes at top and center through which the screws securing the unit to the strut are visible. The recommended strut oil pressure is stencilled in black; the recommended 43-lb pressure for non-tropical versions of the Mk.Vb tires is missing from the stencil at the cover's base.

A close-up of the canopy base shows the portside release cable along the top of the thin red metal strip. When pulled, the cable draws out retention pins above the strip. Elbow pressure on the canopy forces it outward for the slipstream to hurl it clear.

The windshield armored glass panel was originally bolted onto the front, and raised above the frame surface as seen on this Mk. V. It was incorporated into the frame on later production aircraft. Note the rectangular-pattern rear-view mirror.

The white strap attached to the red frame on the canopy front is the canopy release. The thin cable loops down the canopy sides to emerge at the base of the frame.

The support frame comprises vertical channel-sections with lightening holes, linked by two cross tubes, with struts forming an "inverted V" in between. Compensating cylinders with sliding rod inserts control vertical seat adjustments depending on whether it is occupied or empty.

The Spitfire's seat is detached from the cockpit. Frontal view picks out the curved fabric back-rest and shallow pan-base normally occupied by the pilot's parachute, as well as the black lap-belts. The seat is made of molded bakelite with a red-brown texture. Flare cartridges are stored in the rectangular frame fronting the seat-pan base.

An extended view of MH434's rear fuselage picks out the angled separation line with the tail section and the open starboard access panel at the bottom. The open battery hatch to the right exposes its red-colored content.

The seat height adjustment lever is located on the starboard side. The inverted-V frame has six notches into which the lever can be slotted to provide a maximum height variation of four inches. The lever hand-grip is black with a silver front.

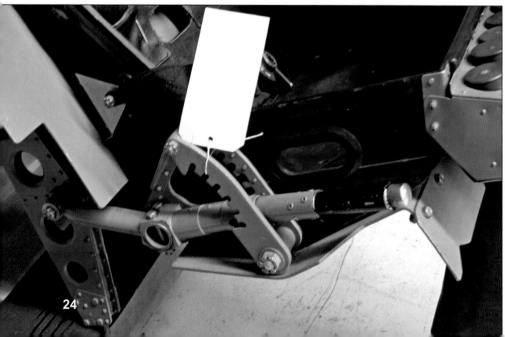

The main control cables link up with flexible lever-arms secured to a tubular frame above and behind the tail wheel shock-absorber strut. These cables operate the elevator (left) and rudder (right). Arms are sprayed Interior grey-green and the strut is silver.

The interim control cable bracket on the Mk. V has the cables for the elevator lever-arm and the lower cable for the rudder lever-arm slotted through its frame. The upper rudder lever-arm cable in the background runs unconstrained along its entire length.

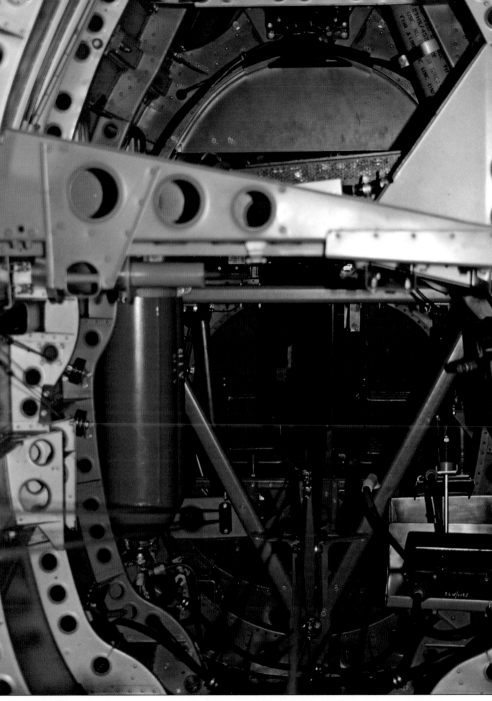

The "V-pattern" tubular support for the pilot's seat is visible in this look forward from the battery hatch. The seat itself is absent, so the two-step rudder pedals can also be seen. On the left is one of two compressed-air cylinders for the aircraft's pneumatic system.

BM597 is a Mk. Vb that bears the Dark earth and Dark green top camouflage applied up to August 1941 when Ocean grey replaced dark earth and Medium sea grey superseded "Sky" underneath. The camouflage extends over the normal dull walkway strip on the wing root.

P9374 has black/white undersides split along the fuselage center line introduced in late 1938 but replaced by "Sky" in mid-1940. Black/white with the port-side roundel outlined in yellow was restored between November 1940 and April 1941. "Sky," and then Medium sea grey took over by August 1941 with the latter retained until VE-Day.

Covering the aperture of the carburetor's air-intake on this Spitfire is a fine mesh screen designed to prevent the ingestion of dirt particles and dust that would adversely affect the carburetor's function.

This nose view of the Mk. V displayed at the Dayton Air Force Museum shows the Vokes filter unit that was applied to Spitfires intended for operations in the desert or similar dust and dirt-laden atmospheres. The bulky shape tended to restrict the aircraft's maximum speed to some degree although overall performance was still sound.

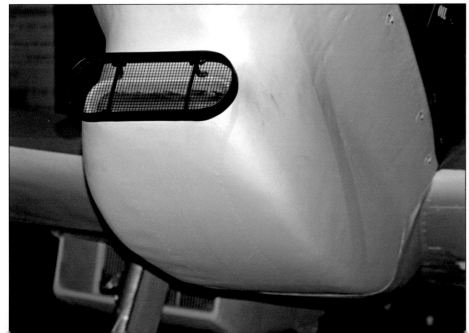

The spinner cover mounted on Mk. V BM597 is extended in length and more streamlined in comparison with Mk. 1 AR213. It is retained in place by a single locking device that is mounted between the two blades in the foreground. Sporting the square red and white Polish national insignia, this aircraft is painted to represent the No. 317 (Wileński) Squadron in honor of the Polish Air Force's part in WWII RAF operations.

The Identification, Friend or Foe (IFF) wires angle inwards to enter the fuselage just behind the radio-hatch in the case of the portside unit. The circular mounting for the entry point is almost at the center of BM597's roundel.

The IFF wires extend forward from the tips of the stabilizer to the fuselage. The rear ends of the wires are secured into brackets mounted on the outer leading edges of the stabilizers.

A closer view of BM597's port stabilizer-tip demonstrates how the IFF wire is secured within a bracket that protrudes from the stabilizer's leading-edge. Deflection of the elevator shows how the aircraft's camouflage-separation line is carried onto the end of the stabilizer.

The fuselage navigation light is housed in an elliptical Plexiglas cover located directly behind the base of the radio mast. It is held in place by a thin metal frame that is secured by rivets. The same fitting on MH434 and PL344 is directly behind the radio mast.

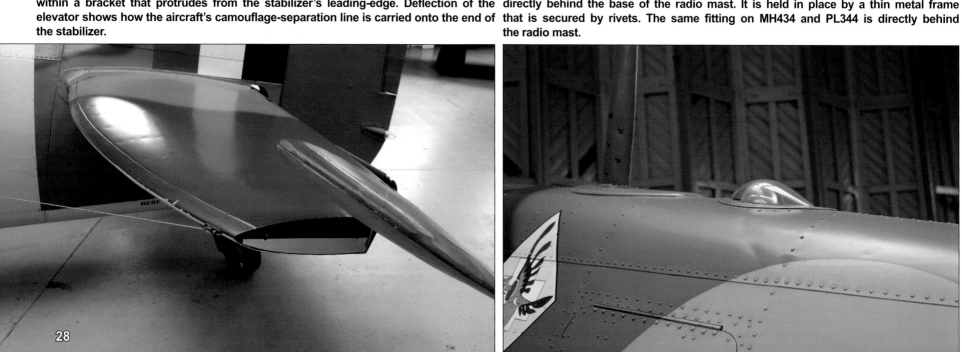

MH434 is a Mk LF IXe variant of R. J. Mitchell's aerodynamically superlative creation. It is based at the Imperial War Museum's airfield at Duxford, England, and is fully airworthy. The code letters ZD relate to No. 222 Squadron whose pilots operated on the type between August 1943 and January 1945.

A complete side-profile view of PL344 reveals the same overall camouflage scheme as that borne by MH434. The removal of Invasion stripes from the top fuselage and wing surfaces was in line with Allied policy once its Armies were established in Normandy.

The four-blade propeller unit first replaced its three-blade predecessor on the Mk. VI Spitfire to become the standard fitting on all Merlin-powered Marks up to the XVI. The blades were constructed either from metal (Dural) or wood (Jablo).

The propeller spinner cover is neatly streamlined but features a small flat profile at the front. The cover is secured in place by twin screws inserted in between the blades and in line with the rear edges of the blade slots.

An air compressor unit is positioned behind and above the starboard rear exhaust stack. The shallow scoop fairing, seen in the center, allows cooling air to be directed onto the compressor.

The Merlin 60-series engine on MH434 displays its six exhaust stacks that are angled outwards, and have expanded circular orifices. They have a burnished metal finish. Stacks on variants up to the Mk. VI had a cowling with three exhaust ports

A noteworthy feature of the PR Spitfire (as distinct from the standard fighter variants) is its frameless windshield, as seen on this fine example of a PR Mk. XI Spitfire in the USAF Museum. The overall color of this aircraft is Cerulean or PR Blue, intended to disguise the aircraft's image at high altitude.

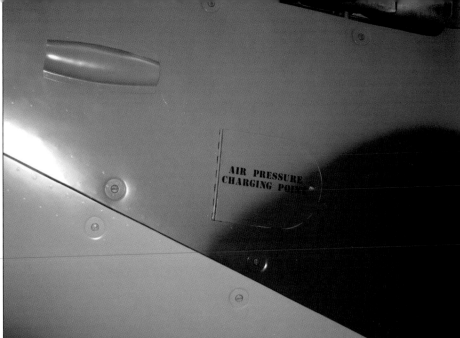

The lettering on the air pressure charging point panel is applied in black; the D-pattern panel is secured by a single screw. The small air-scoop at the top left directs cooling air onto the generator

The carburetor air-intake cover extends beyond the wing leading-edges, compared to previous variants, whose forward end was marginally behind the wing leading edges. However, photo evidence exists of Mk IXs with the shorter-length fairing.

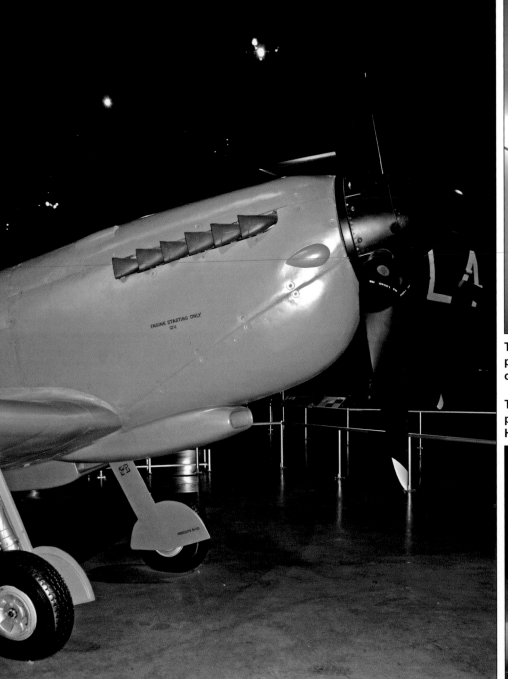

The standard curved pattern of the Spitfire's lower engine cowling has given way to the much more angular shape seen on the USAF Museum's PR Mk. XI. The change was deemed necessary in order to accommodate a larger oil-tank for this variant to fly long-range sorties.

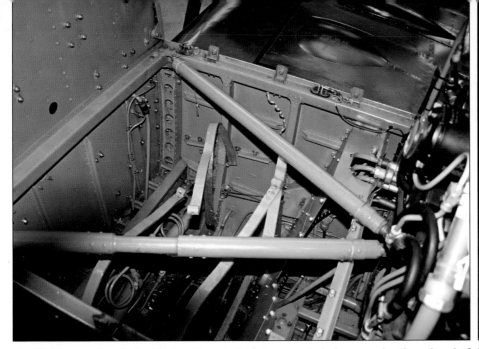

The Spitfire carries its fuel in two "header" tanks mounted above each other ahead of the cockpit in the compartment seen here. The V-pattern rods are detachable in order to gain access for the lower (37-Imperial-Gallon-capacity) tank.

This is the larger of the two "header" fuel tanks for the Spitfire, which has a capacity of 48 Imperial Gallons. It is positioned in the upper section of the compartment. The surface is sprayed in Interior grey-green.

The Spitfire's radio hatch is positioned directly behind the cockpit frame. The four base and side-support frames all feature lightening holes. The fuselage interior is sprayed in Interior grey-green.

The radio hatch door is retained in the open position by a single strut mounted on the front end. The white writing on a red background states the fighter must either have the radio or an equivalent weight placed inside before it can be taken into the air.

WARNING
THIS AIRCRAFT
MUST NOT BE
FLOWN WITHOUT
WIRELESS OR
EQUIVALENT
BALLAST

The radio hatch door is here secured in place on MH434. Stencilled in black is a warning that the interior must contain either the radio or an equivalent weight in ballast. The First Aid wording is applied in red.

The Spitfire's original aerial mast, a thin, untapered rod, was replaced by this vertically tapered unit. A saddle-pattern lug with twin holes is positioned at the top-rear of the mast. The fuselage identification light is directly behind the mast-base.

The Spitfire's battery hatch is positioned ahead of the starboard stabilizer. It is hinged at the base and secured at the top by three screws. The stencilled letters BATTERY are applied in black

A regular feature on RAF fighters from November 1940 was the application of a color band ahead of the stabilizers that was finished in "Sky S." The official dimension was 18 inches but PL344's band appears broader.

The Mk. XVI Spitfire's top fuselage behind the cockpit was cut down and the normal canopy was replaced by a "bubble"-design that afforded an enhanced degree of visibility, especially to the rear as evident here.

The Spitfire's "C" Wing had provision for two cannon-mounts, in contrast to the "B" Wing's single mount.

"C" Wing

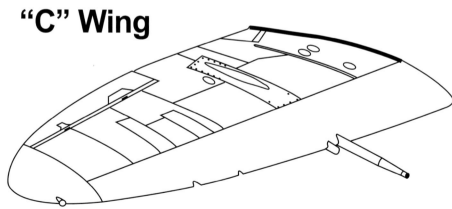

A vertical signal cartridge launcher unit is mounted in the top-rear fuselage ahead of the "Sky S"-band. It is positioned to starboard of the aircraft center-line and the aperture is covered by a red doped patch.

The MK IX's tail-wheel is non-retractable. The angled upper strut section seen on PL344 is fixed, but the lower section swivels, allowing the wheel to castor through 360 degrees. Recommended oil pressure for the strut is stencilled in black.

The tail wheel strut extends through the bulkhead to link up with the shock-absorber strut. Removal of the ballast compartment panel directly above the strut on MH434 reveals a series of four circular weights that act as a counter-weight.

A view of the other side of PL344's tail wheel picks out the recommended air pressure stencilled above the camouflage separation line. The ribbed tread on the wheel-surface was not a standard feature during WWII, when plain surfaces were the norm.

The tail-wheel was non-retractable up to the Mk. VII. The same retractable modification on the Mk. VIII was applied to the PR Mk. XI as seen on the USAF Museum's MB950 that flew in England with the 14 Photo Squadron.

A second view of the tail-wheel strut on MH434 reveals how it is attached to the bulkhead frame. The circular mounting at the top houses the pivot spindle. The absent wheel bracket exposes the tapered end of the wheel pivot unit. "Jack Here" is stencilled in black.

The black dotted W/T stencil is one of several applied, for example, to the areas around the flight controls. These markings relate to the bonding of the controls to the airframe to prevent static-electricity build-up as well as giving enhanced radio transmission and reception. The small rod atop the rudder is the rear connector for the radio aerial wire.

With the tail-wheel detached on MH434 the U-pattern support bracket is fully visible. Also displayed is the circular pivot mount in between the support bracket and the base of the tail-wheel strut.

The starboard side of the Spitfire's fin has an angular cut-out whose forward edge also forms part of the fin rear spar. It houses part of the rudder trim-tab mechanism. The cover plate is secured by screws.

The original fin and rudder pattern applied to the Spitfire and featured here on MH434 was elliptical in overall shape. Some Mk. IX rudders were replaced with the elongated and more pointed units that were first introduced on the Mark VII variant.

MH434's rudder has been detached. The trim-tab rod angles out left from its slot in the flanged channel into which the detached rudder normally slots. Also seen are the rudder hinge brackets along with their securing pins.

The rudder hinge line is vertical up to the top rib, from where it goes forward horizontally. A 3½-lb. mass-balance is in the forward tip. The maximum deflection is 28 degrees either way. The surface is covered in doped fabric.

A circular inspection panel is mounted on the lower port side of the vertical fin. The cable just visible at the base of the panel is part of the rudder trim-tab control mechanism. It runs over a pulley positioned to the right of the aperture.

The rudder actuating rod is mounted on the port side of the fuselage. The rear end is attached to the large bracket frame mounted on the rudder. The rod is channelled forward into a triangular metal trough.

The rudder trim-tab is positioned in the center of the frame. The actuating rod is fitted on the starboard side and runs forward into a metal channel that is secured by small screws. Maximum deflection is 6 degrees to starboard but is 18 degrees to port

The Spitfire's elevators are similar in pattern to the rudder. Metal-framed trim-tabs are fitted along the center of the trailing edges and the surfaces are covered in doped fabric. The angular cut-out on the inner edge permits full rudder deployment

The elevator trim-tabs are activated by rods attached to the top of curved metal frames located towards the tab's inner edge. The rods have triangular-pattern metal covers. The tabs have a maximum 20-degree upward and 7-degree downward deflection.

The tail navigation light is located directly below the trim-tab. The support frame for the clear-glass bulb is elliptical and held in place by six screws on either side of the frame.

The forward outer edge of the elevator, seen here from below, angles up to meet the outer tip section. The elevators have a 28-degree upward and 23-degree downward movement. An inspection panel on the stabilizer accesses the elevator trim-tab screw-jack.

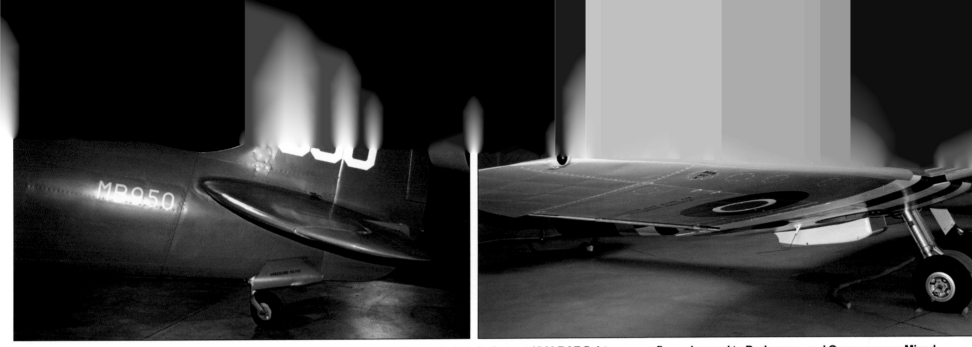

The original fin-and-rudder structure was amended on several variants that included the PR Mk. XI. The increased area of the rudder in particular provided the pilot with enhanced manoevering-power and stability.

The Mk. IX's main navigation lights are fitted into circular mountings that protrude from the wing-tips. The bulbs are green (starboard) and red (port). Later variants from the Mk. XIV onwards featured Plexiglas covers flush with the wing leading edges.

In August 1941 RAF fighter camouflage changed to Dark green and Ocean grey or Mixed grey above with Sea grey medium underneath. Yellow stripes on the outer wing leading edges gave a visual indicator to ground crew working in the dark.

Red doped patches were applied over machine gun apertures to prevent dirt and dust gaining access prior to the weapons being fired in combat. The outer aperture is positioned slightly higher than the inner aperture.

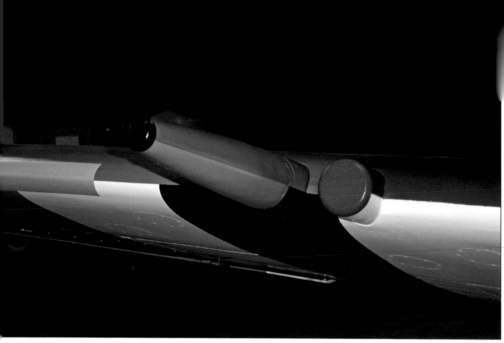

The cannon barrels are covered by neat fairings on PL344 but short length and smooth surface suggests that these examples are replicas. The camouflage separation line is applied to the fairing sides. The inside fairing-base bears a red-sprayed cap.

This is the port cannon fairing on MH434. It features extra length and a two-section configuration. Each section is retained in place by screws, with a "collar" fitting where the fairing links up with the wing structure.

Three of the series of circular access panels positioned on the underside of each wing directly behind the wing leading edges, are seen here. There is another circular access panel behind and in line with the outside stencilled panel.

Detachment of the wing/fuselage fairing reveals five of the six curved formers that act as a support for this component, which is divided between five panels; the rear pair are conjoined, whether fitted or detached.

The black cap positioned above and behind the port trailing edge accesses the ground socket for the Spitfire's radio and electrical systems. The socket is normally enclosed within the wing's rear fairing panel.

The removal of the panels from the Spitfire's main armament bay shows the twin apertures for the cannon-caliber weapons. Only single examples were fitted in general however. Also exposed is the bay for the inner machine-gun.

The fairing's absence provides a view of the inner-flap interior and the roller bar that activates this flight control sub-unit. The separation with the outer flap can just be discerned on the wing trailing edge inboard of the screw-holes for the fairing panel.

MH434's wing walk-way surfaces have circular access points on the forward section. The single example at the front provides entry to the top of the landing gear. The pair of holes behind accesses the radiator's inlet and outlet pipe fittings.

The flaps have been dropped and the port flap visual indicator on MH434 is now raised in the exposed position. The cover is hinged on its inner rim and is automatically pushed up by the deployment of the indicator.

MH434 bears the standard black line stencil on the upper wings. The words Walkway Inboard is a warning to avoid stepping onto the major part of the wing surface containing the gun hatches that were thin and less capable of bearing weight.

The cannon bay panel has a raised streamlined fairing in the center whose interior accommodates the greater bulk of the circular ammunition feed drum. The panel to the outside covers the cannon's ammunition container.

The flap visual indicator is located just behind and inboard of the cannon fairing. It is seen in the closed position; when raised up it acts as a confirmation that the flaps are lowered. Initial production airframes were equipped with double units.

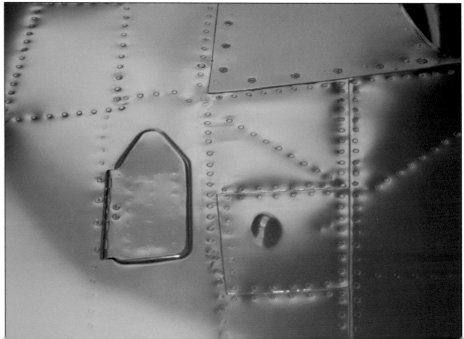

The two aileron hinge-points are covered by raised plates on the top aileron surface. This is the starboard-inner fitting that is the larger of the two and features a three-side shape. Access to the hinges is gained via the underside of the aileron.

The aileron outer-hinge cover plate is small in scale and features a curved inside edge. Both hinge covers are part of the forward aileron section, whose seam is raised along its full length.

The fabric-covered ailerons on Mk. 1 and Mk. 2 Spitfires imposed inordinate physical strain on pilots in combat. The light-alloy, metal-covered ailerons introduced on the Mk. V and onwards, made for easier handling.

The dotted lines and wording directly above MH434's landing gear bay are applied in orange and spaced wider apart than the red-applied lines on the Mk. V. They encompass both the "teardrop" bulge and the slim inner weapon bay fairing.

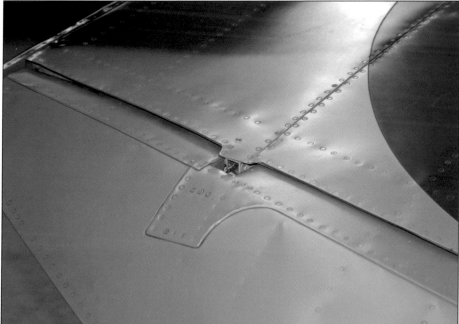

The Spitfire's flaps extend from the ailerons to the fuselage sides. This overall view shows the port-side flap in the fully-open position that is also the sole angle of deployment other than when in the closed position. The individual ribs are attached to the roller bar.

Each flap unit is split at a point just outboard of the fuselage. A thin metal rod links the two sections. The inner section has an angled trailing edge in order for it to fit flush with the flat inner wing surface.

A view of MH434's starboard-outer wing section demonstrates the slim nature of the aileron that is in keeping with the Spitfire's overall aesthetic layout. The roundel's red element highlights the ovoid bulge that accommodates the securing pin for the rear stirrup retaining the outer machine gun in place. The Mk. V's equivalent cover seen on page 16 is a slim "ridge" pattern.

The "E Wing" had the same fire-power as the "C Wing," but the "active" cannon barrel was applied to the outside stub rather than the inner location on the "C Wing."

"E" Wing

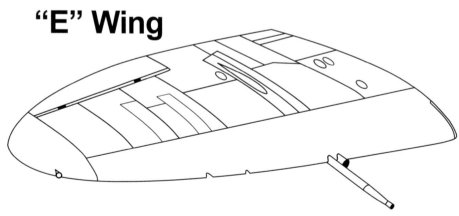

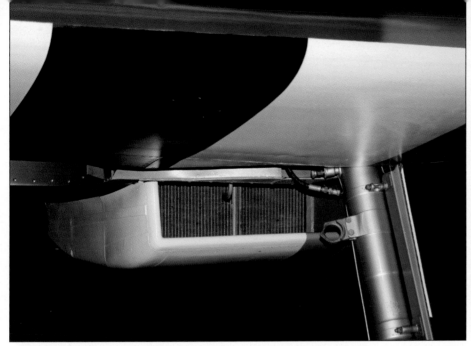

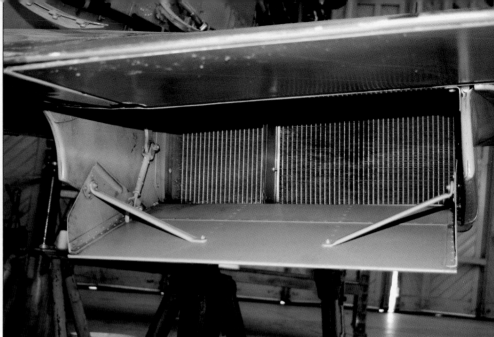

The Mk. IX possesses radiator units, housed in rectangular fairings, under both inner-wing surfaces. The port unit that also houses the oil-cooler equipment replaced the small circular cover for the oil-cooler from the Mk VII onwards.

The starboard radiator cover has a neat overall outline. It is held in place by screws mounted in the flanged outer strips. The panel alongside the forward section accesses the radiator's outer retention pin prior to detaching the unit.

The radiator flap is here fully lowered. A lever on the inner surface controls the flap deployment, while two laterally-fixed bracing rods protect the sides of the flap from airflow buffeting. The interior color appears to match the Sea grey-medium undersides.

The Spitfire's 90-Gallon belly tank had a center-front recess that slotted neatly over the carburetor intake cover. The tank could be jettisoned.

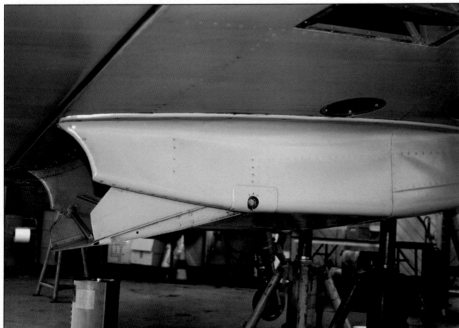

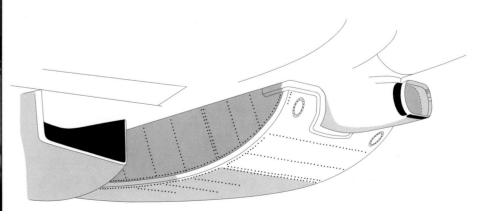

The port-side radiator block with its silver external skin is fully exposed on MH434. The more bulky structure replaced the narrow oil-cooler unit fitted to variants of the Spitfire as far as the HF Mk. VI.

When detached, the machine gun bay panels expose the wing-frame structure. The hinged panel on the left normally acts as the base for both ammunition boxes, which are inserted laterally, with the forward box feeding the inner weapon and rear box the outer weapon.

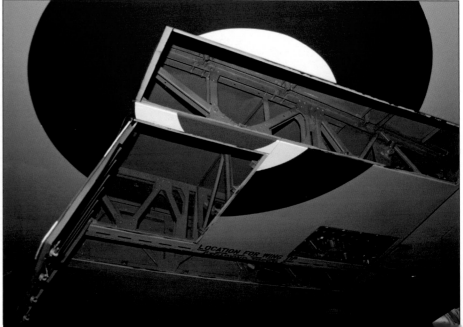

The Spitfire's pitot-mast is located under the port wing, alongside the inner support trestle stencil. The vertical section is covered by a parallel-sided streamlined sheath that is tapered at the base. The unit slots into the side of the access panel surround.

The hinged panel that forms the base for the ammunition box is secured shut by levers attached to the inner-screw mountings. The Type C roundel's white band is too wide as laid down in RAF WWII instructions.

Each wing tip consists of a metal main rib and spar with the other ribs and formers made of spruce. The protruding nuts for the two securing bolts are clearly visible. The navigation light covers in MH434's case extend over the inner half of the frames.

The Spitfire has two stencils under each wing where trestles are placed whenever the aircraft is raised up off its landing gear. This outer stencil on PL344's starboard wing is applied in black lettering.

This close look at MH434's wing tip section picks out the raised strip on the leading edge in line with the tip's separation line. The un-tapered yellow strip contrasts with the tapered strip on PL344, although both variations can be seen on WWII Spitfires.

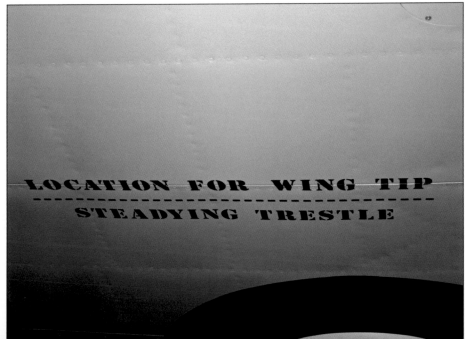

This side view of the windshield reveals how the armored Plexiglas fits within the structure, and the joint line where the windshield frame links up with the rear frame cross-strip. The mirror base straddles the front and rear frames.

A rearward view from a marginal side-angle emphasizes the distinctive bulge in the sliding canopy's overall shape. This feature afforded the pilot more head-room than he had in the original frame, whose top rim was in line with the rear fuselage.

The windshield comprises an angled-back metal frame curved at the top. Two horizontal strips link it to the rear frame that is also curved at the top. The base is formed of convex-curved strips. The inside is sprayed in Interior grey-green.

MH434 has a circular rear-view mirror, an absolutely vital item to give warning of encroaching enemy aircraft. Many airframes up to the Mk. V bore a rectangular mirror inside a deep-sided metal cover during the 1940-1941 period of operations.

The pilot's head-rest consists of a round leather pad finished in black that is attached to the top of the triangular frame. The seat harness straps are fed through a slit located in the center of the frame.

The twin circular containers, whose nearside sections are linked by a solid metal strip, hold the voltage regulator equipment. The unit is bolted to the bulkhead behind the pilot's seat, in line with the head-rest.

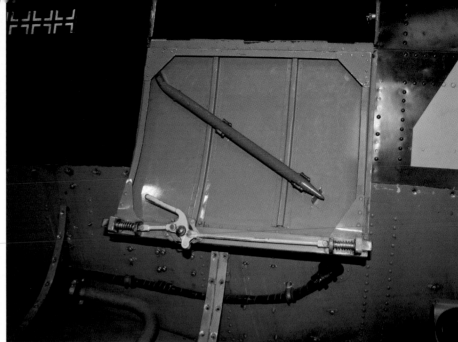

Spitfires are fitted with a small port-side door that hinges downward. The door locking/unlocking mechanism is finished in yellow. The red crowbar secured by flexible metal clips is for emergency use, should a canopy jam shut.

No. 74 (Tiger) Squadron's insignia dates back to the unit's creation during WWI. It is applied to both lower-rear sides of the engine cowling. The predator's head is mounted inside a white circle that is, in turn, inside a yellow-edged, black "arrow-head."

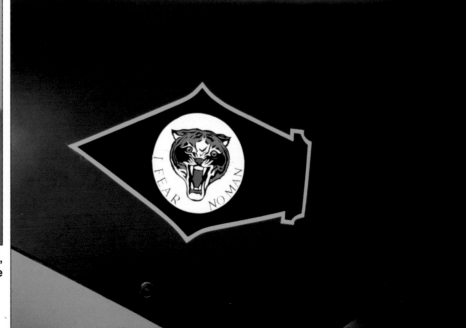

The "inverted-L" handle with silver finish on its horizontal section is the engine throttle. The black propeller control lever is directly to the right. The large black wheel with knurled surface directly behind is the elevator trim with the smaller black wheel adjusting the rudder.

The silver cylinder with connecting yellow-topped black cables positioned on the port-side floor operates the radiator flaps. Equipment housed in the black and silver frames are modern installations and therefore not part of the standard equipment in a WWII Spitfire.

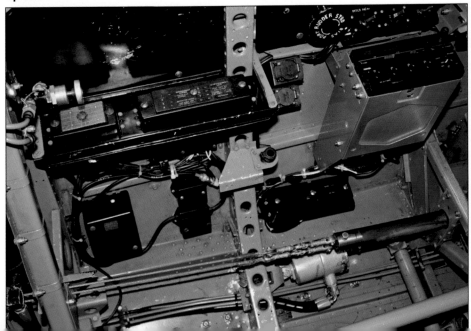

A close-up of the reflector gun-sight picks out the supports for the angled reflector glass and the Sorbo pad that protects the pilot from violent impact with the sight base. Bolts secure the two-part circular clamp that holds the gun-sight in place.

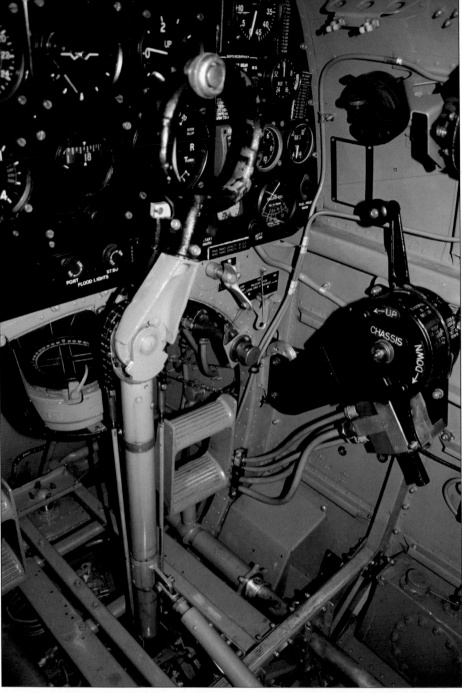

The left-hand instrument panel with the red flap-lever at the top directly ahead of the throttle console contains the oxygen regulator directly below the lever. Oxygen-content dial is top right while the aircraft flight-angle dial is at bottom right. The dial at the center-bottom of the panel indicates the brake pressure level.

The control column comprises a vertically-aligned rod to which is attached a flexible upper section topped by a "spade" pattern hand-grip. The chain seen attached to the front of the flexible upper-section is linked to thin rods that extend down the sides of the column to its base.

The elevator-actuation rod is attached to the control-column base by a "yoke" that is secured in place using a threaded bolt with hexagonal nuts. The knurled wheel seen on the starboard rudder shaft allows for the foot-rest to be suitably adjusted in length.

The original rudder-pedals had one foot-rest. The double foot-rest was introduced after test comparison with a captured Bf 109 whose more rearward-angled seat allowed the pilot to bear higher G-forces. The adaptation was a success.

The blind-flying panel with the standard six dials takes up the bulk of the center section of the MH 434's main instrument panel. Engine and fuel-monitoring dials and gauges are mounted on the right-side.

On the top row of the blind-flying panel dials are (L-R) the airspeed indicator, artificial horizon, and climb/descent rate. The altimeter is seen through the "spade" hand-grip with the directional gyro and turn-and-bank indicator alongside. The panel is black.

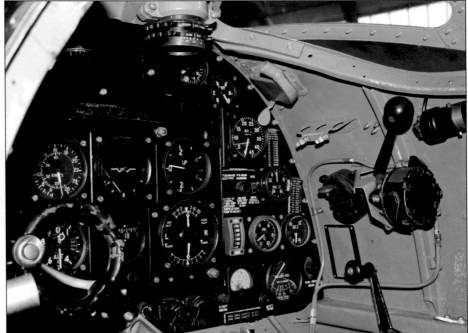

dial at the top of the starboard panel is the engine RPM counter with the red-rimmed
st gauge below. The rectangular orange unit is the oil pressure gauge in line with the
il content and black-rimmed coolant temperature gauges. The fuel gauge is at the
r-base with the red-backed fuel pressure warning indicator on the right.

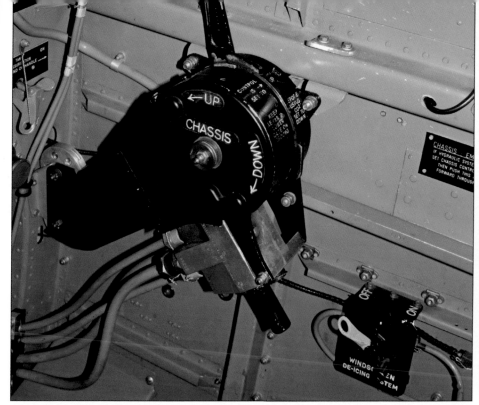

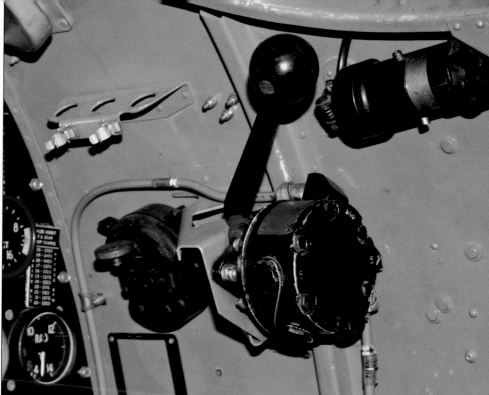

The landing-gear control unit is in a circular black frame on the starboard wall. The outer cover's wording advises keeping the lever in the lower gate while on the ground. Inner cover wording advises a "down" lever position before using the CO_2. The black box with yellow handle contains the windshield de-icing controls

The wobble pump is mounted on the starboard cockpit frame directly above the landing-gear control unit. The pump's primary function is for priming the carburetor as part of the start-up process. Improper lever-operation can delay start-up by flooding the carburetor chamber.

A Mk. XVI with its distinctive bubble-canopy and bearing No. 421 (Canadian) Squadron codes is flanked by a Hurricane and a Mk. IV Mustang. All are powered by the Rolls-Royce Merlin.

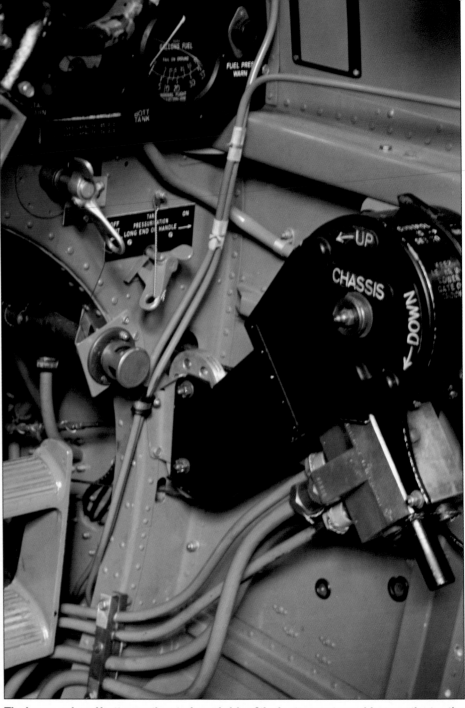

MH434's control column hand-grip has the gun button at top left. The light orange button has a silver milled surround that rotates to two positions, "Fire" and "Safe"; the hand-grip surface is black. The brake lever is mounted ahead of the hand-grip base.

The brass-colored button on the starboard side of the instrument panel-base activates the engine priming pump. The fuel cock control lever is top left and fuel tank pressurization switch is directly below the black instruction panel.

The revised operating switch for a fighter equipped with cannon and machine guns is seen here. The rectangular silver frame replaces the button-pattern unit as applied to MH434's hand-grip. The switch also operates the gun camera.

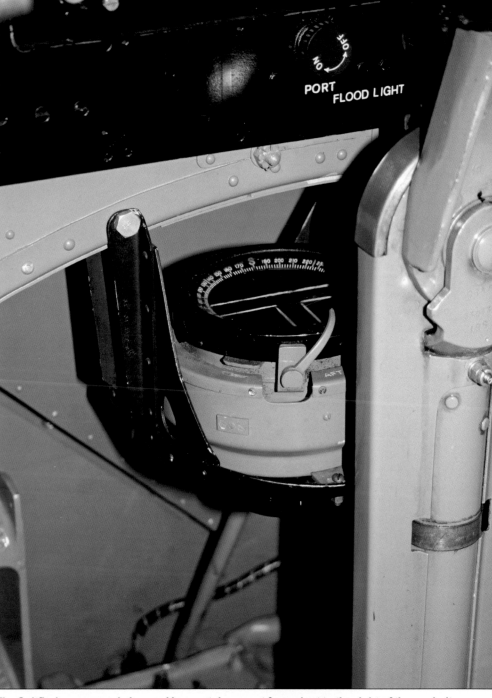

The Spitfire's compass is housed in a metal support frame just to the right of the cockpit center-line. The black frame is secured to the lower bulkhead by hexagonal nuts. The compass casing is finished in a shade of gray akin to Sea grey medium.

Spitfire Mk IXc Specifications

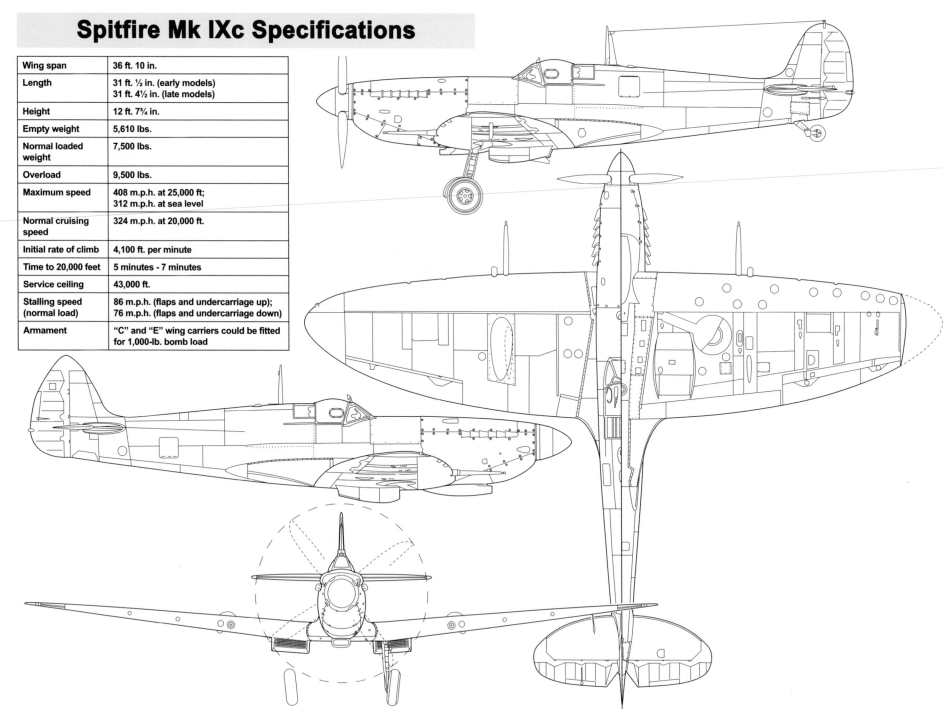

Wing span	36 ft. 10 in.
Length	31 ft. ½ in. (early models) 31 ft. 4½ in. (late models)
Height	12 ft. 7¾ in.
Empty weight	5,610 lbs.
Normal loaded weight	7,500 lbs.
Overload	9,500 lbs.
Maximum speed	408 m.p.h. at 25,000 ft; 312 m.p.h. at sea level
Normal cruising speed	324 m.p.h. at 20,000 ft.
Initial rate of climb	4,100 ft. per minute
Time to 20,000 feet	5 minutes - 7 minutes
Service ceiling	43,000 ft.
Stalling speed (normal load)	86 m.p.h. (flaps and undercarriage up); 76 m.p.h. (flaps and undercarriage down)
Armament	"C" and "E" wing carriers could be fitted for 1,000-lb. bomb load

The Spitfire's landing gear retracts outward. The landing-gear struts are located close to the fuselage, making for a narrow track of 5 ft. 8 in. that caused problems with directional stability particularly when landing.

The landing-gear struts are angled slightly forward. The curved front-section of the stream-lined Duralumin cover, which extends down to the wheel hub, overlaps the wheel diameter. The lower wheel section remains exposed when the gear is retracted.

This head-on view shows how the axle of the vertically-aligned oleo-pneumatic shock-absorber strut is marginally angled downwards so as to create an inward tilt of the wheel. The strut cover has a "wrap-around" curve along its lower length.

The front pair of lugs for attaching the landing-gear cover are visible on the top section of the strut. On the inner-top surface is also the large lug whose circular portion retains the wheel in place when retracted. The air valve filler plug is directly above the lug.

This wheel hub has three wedge-shaped "lightening" cut-outs within the concave frame. Three centrally-positioned bolts on the inner-surface secure the frame. The oleo-strut's oil pressure figure is applied in black at the top. The strut slots into the cover's central recess.

Detachment of the wheel provides a full view of the anti-torque frame in front of the strut's oleo-section. Air pressure acts as a shock-absorber with oil providing the damping medium that lessens the rebound effect. The wheel drum is secured by six threaded bolts on the inner facing.

A more frontal view of the starboard landing-gear strut reveals the braided surface of the wheel drum. The lower lug for the securing screw of the landing gear cover is above the anti-torque frame. The thin metal locking rod extends up to the oil-filler plug.

The landing-gear strut slots into the narrow parallel-sided gap in the wing surface. The oil filler plug is at the base of the tapered lever arm that links with the outer end of the hydraulic piston.

Rear-angle view of the starboard wheel bay on MH434 picks out the pair of fore-and-aft channelled strip-frames spanning the roof. The strip center-sections lie flush with the bay roof. The main wing-spar runs across the front of the bay.

The landing gear wheel bay is circular in shape and is larger in diameter than the wheel in order to accommodate the forward edge of the wheel cover-base. The interior surface is sprayed in Interior grey-green.

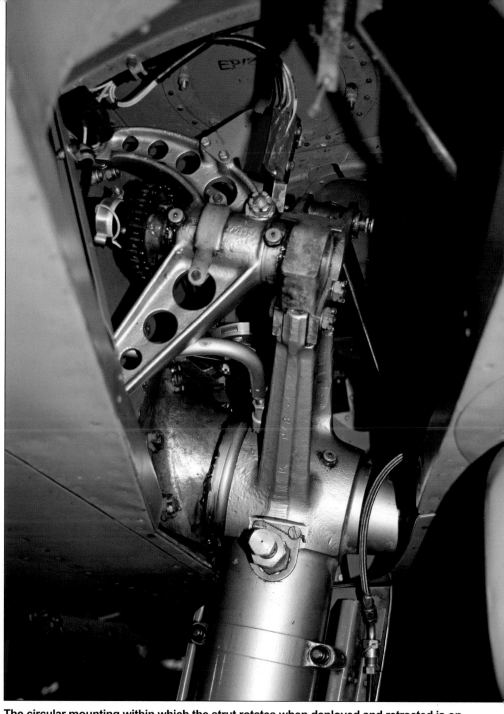

The circular mounting within which the strut rotates when deployed and retracted is on the left. The curved lever frame (top left) is fixed to the bay leading edge and linked in the center to the strut lever arm. A silver brake cable (right) channels down the gear cover.

The Mk. IX had the Merlin 60 Series power-plant with a two-stage supercharger unit. This feature, and a power up-rate between 100 and 170 h.p. compared to the Merlin 45/50 Series, enabled the Mk. IX to wrest back aerial superiority from the Fw 190, whose overall performance, other than in the turn, had seriously exceeded that of the Mk. V.

The Spitfire's oil tank is positioned under the forward section of the engine. It has a fluid capacity of 8.5 Gallons with an additional 1.4 Imperial Gallons air-space. A silver drain-plug is fitted at the rear of the tank base. The unit is sprayed in Interior grey-green.

MH434's propeller spinner cover is detached to expose the hub. The propeller pitch-control unit's cover is finished in Grey and the base is shiny Black as are the propeller blades, but the blade retaining "collars" are burnished in texture. The base-plate, which has numerous lightening holes, is sprayed in Interior grey-green.

The Spitfire's coolant tank is located directly behind the propeller base-plate. The contents are comprised of a 70% distilled water and 30% ethylene-glycol mix. The tank exterior is light silver with a burnished metal filler-cap.

A view of the starboard nose area picks out the right-hand pipe in Interior grey-green through which the coolant tank's glycol is channelled. The tank is positioned directly above the engine's reduction-gear casing.

The generator on MH434's engine is positioned on the forward port-side section of the engine block and immediately above the top of the engine-bearer frame. Its circular exterior is sprayed in Mid-grey.

MH434's carburetor air-intake cover has here been restored. The trunking is marginally raised in the center section. The entire unit will be enclosed by the shaped lower cowling frame. This extended version of the cover was introduced on the Mk. VIII Spitfire.

The detached carburetor intake cover reveals the fuselage inlet frame, secured by screws set into the flanged base. The jack-points are mounted on the main wing-spar attachment frames. Fuel-tank sump and shut-off valve are accessed via the apertures behind the inlet frame.

The Mk IX's detached carburetor air-intake cover has a slim outline. The inside is sprayed Interior grey-green.

Eight lock nuts link up the two tubular lengths of the engine bearer frame to a rectangular retention frame. Twin frame end-mounts slot over the lug on the firewall, with a threaded bolt securing the sub-unit.

Positioned on the engine port-side between the two vertical strengthening frames is a dark rectangular unit with X-patterns on its surface. This unit contains the radio suppression equipment.

The broad parallel-sided frame with flanged edges and lightening holes extends between the top and lower tubular lengths, to provide extra strength to the rear of the engine bearer frame.

An echelon-right formation of 65 Squadron Mk. I Spitfires display several features on the original variant. The markings are restricted to Type B fuselage and upper-wing roundels. The parallel-sided radio mast would give way to a tapered equivalent. Similarly, the fork-pattern pitot-mast would be replaced by a single unit.

Flight Lt. Clouston was leading a line-astern Section when his No. 19 Squadron Mk I received this normally catastrophic degree of damage. He nevertheless brought off a forced-landing on Newmarket race-course. His aircraft has no fin flash, a feature only introduced in May 1940, and the aircraft letter W applied lower than the Squadron code.

Seven Mk. Vbs from No. 417 (RCAF) Squadron all bear Vokes air-filter units as they over-fly Tunisian soil in mid-1943. The aircraft in the foreground displays the Dark earth and Mid-stone top camouflage applied to MTO units. The loose formation being flown would reduce the chances of being "bounced" by Axis fighters.

A Mk V Spitfire with its lower engine cowling panels detached undergoes a test at full power. The airmen packed onto the stabilizers act as a deterrent to the tail lifting off under the airflow. The 64 Squadron fighter's serial number appears obliterated by the "Sky S" rear fuselage band. This unit was the first to switch to the Mk IX in mid-1942.

The 31FG was allocated a number of Mk. VIII and IX Spitfires. Lt. Griffin stands by the nose of a 307FS Mk. IX. The pilots were initially unhappy when the Group transferred onto P-51s in early 1944 but soon realized the "Spit" had no practical function in providing long-range escorts for the 15USAAF B-17s and B-24s.

Two pilots of West Indian background are posed alongside a Mk. V Spitfire. Both wear late-pattern RAF flying boots. The wheel has a solid hub-cover. What was probably an insignia or reference to the squadron has evidently been deleted from the lower engine cowling.

The smashed blades and flattened oil-cooler on the upturned port wing bear witness to the operational demise of a Mk. Vb, bearing 52FG codes. The aircraft is surrounded by other smashed or dismantled airframes on this North African airfield. VF: D is recorded as being "written off" during July 1943.

The tapered wing and retractable tail wheel are pointers to the aircraft being a Mk VIII, in this case a HF (high-level flight) variant. It is running up to full power with the airman on the rear fuselage acting as a counter-weight. The aircraft belongs to 92 Squadron that was based in Italy between September 1943 and VE-Day.

The Mk. VI was the first of two successive Marks developed for high-altitude operations. A pressurised cockpit and extended wings with pointed tips were features. The thin strake below the exhaust stubs houses the air intake for the Merlin 47's pressurizing system. There are five wedge-pattern cut-outs within the wheel hub-cover.

Demonstrating that the phrase "sunny Italy" was an ironic misnomer especially in wintertime, a party of ground personnel struggle to move their Mk. VIII charge from the cloying grip of the very muddy Advanced Airfield surface in 1943.

Geoffrey Page, CO of No. 125 (Fighter) Wing, taxies his bomb-laden Mk. IXe for a sortie against German ground units. His initials AGP applied in "Sky S" under the nose are repeated on the fuselage. Reduced D-Day stripes indicate picture was taken some weeks after D-Day. The castoring tail-wheel is here in reversed position.

The spiritual needs of RAF personnel in the field were not ignored. A padre (second right at front) oversees the un-loading of a portable musical instrument at Bazenville in France that was occupied by No. 421 Squadron's Mk. IXs from June to August 1944.

The distinctive plan outline of the Spitfire is caught as what appears to be a Mk. XI or Mk. XIII, to judge by the twin camera ports under the portside fuselage, banks away. Of the four PR Merlin-engine variants, only the Mk. XIII carried any armament, limited to four machine-guns, but their presence cannot be discerned here.

A ground crewman serving with the 31FG at San Severo or Mondolfo in Italy inspects the smashed propeller unit on this Mk. IX Spitfire from an unidentified squadron "Type C" upper wing roundels indicate the picture was taken no earlier than 1945 when these markings displaced their red/blue "Type B" predecessors.

This Mk. I Spitfire is parked at Upland airfield near Ottowa, Canada, in September 1939. The reduced-size Type B roundel is unusual, but the lack of a fin-flash, the un-tapered mast, and the serial L1090 on the upper fin are typical of early-production airframes.

A Mk. VIII Spitfire lifts off with the main landing gear adopting a "knock-kneed" configuration as it retracts. The tail wheel is already fully retracted. The absence of Squadron codes prevents unit identification.

This Mk. Vb /R6923 now assigned to No. 92 (East India) Squadron was originally a cannon-armed Mk.1a flown by No. 19 Squadron in 1940; it was brought up to Mk. V standard in early 1941 and is being flown by the CO, S/Ldr. Jamie Rankin

A line-up of No. 136 Squadron's Mk. VIII Spitfires is seen at its airfield on the Cocos Islands in the Indian Ocean some time between March and October 1945. Reduced-size code letters and two-tone blue South East Asia Command (SEAC) National markings are points of note.

MH434 is photographed at an Airshow during a stage in her post-War existence when she bore full D-Day stripes. However, the AC unit codes are not applicable to any RAF Fighter Command Squadron operating during WWII.

MK356 is a Mk. IX fitted with the pointed fin and rudder structure. Her camouflage scheme has given way to a silver finish and she bears the UF codes for No. 601 (Auxiliary) Sqdn. She is seen landing off a display at a 2012 Airshow held at Duxford near Cambridge.

The IWM's airfield at Duxford, England, forms the backcloth for AR501, a Shuttleworth Trust Mk. V. The codes relate to 310 (Czechoslovakian) Squadron. That unit operated as part of the Duxford Wing during the Battle of Britain but actually flew Hurricanes from the satellite airfield at Fowlmere.

A Mk. Vb Spitfire, serving with No. 243 Squadron, flies at an uncomfortably short distance from the photographer's aerial platform, but provides a detailed image for the viewer. The serial No. (ER821) is mainly concealed by the tail color-band. The aircraft letter is applied lower than the unit letters on the starboard fuselage but this layout is reversed on the port-side.